Simple Thoughts About Life & Living

Glenn Poveromo

Cricket Cottage Publishing

Copyright 2013 Cricket Cottage Publishing. All rights reserved, Printed in the United States of America. Excerpts as permitted under the United States Act of 1976, no part of the publication may be reproduced or distributed in any form or by any means, or stored in a database or retrieval system, without the prior written permission of the publisher.

For information about group sales and permission, contact Cricket Cottage Publishing, LLC, 1889 South Kirkman Road, Suite 614, Orlando, Florida 32811 or call 407-255-7785.

Website: www.thecricketpublishing.com

ISBN: 978-0615912295
ISBN-10: 061591229X

Dedication

This book is dedicated to my beautiful family and to all those who are seeking to live their best life possible. I wish you all Peace, Love, & a Smile in your Heart!

Testimonials

I am visually impaired, and have been receiving Glenn's words of wisdom for the past three years. His words of encouragement sometimes feel like he is writing directly to me. His messages have come at a time when they are most needed. I often pass his messages on to my students, who greatly appreciate them. I can only wish that more people would follow his example. Thank you, Glenn, and keep up the great work.

Devin Fernandez, Third Eye Insight, West Islip, NY

Simple Thoughts About Life and Living has helped me because I sometimes have a tendency to look at the worst side of a scenario. Whenever I read Glenn Poveromo's simple thoughts about life, it always makes me realize that there is a better way to look at things…He helps me to see that: "The glass is half full instead of half empty."

Joel E. Eisen, Boca Raton, FL

Glenn's *Simple Thoughts About Life & Living* messages are part psychological, part biblical, and part homespun. They are always entertaining and are part of my day. They are my daily pep talk. Thank you, Glenn.

Joe Coords, San Diego, CA

Words cannot express how much I look forward to Glenn's *Simple Thoughts About Life & Living*. They are such a positive jumpstart to my day. It definitely makes me think and feel better about everything. It's a positive light in a busy world and it's amazing that the more I read them, the more I apply it to my life. I would be very happy to purchase such an uplifting book. Thank you, Glenn.

Sincerely, Maria Cacioppo

Simple Thoughts has served as a great way to start my day over the past several years. The wisdom that they provide has been priceless and profound, yet always "simple". As I have told you, Glenn, the challenge is always to put them into practice. They have helped in improving my "day-to-day" and therefore my life. Thank you so much....

Dan Benjamin

Each morning, I look forward to the *Simple Thoughts about Life and Living* emails. So many of them resonate with me and I enjoy forwarding them to friends and family. I've turned many people on to Glenn and they also look forward to reading his thoughts. *Simple Thoughts About Life & Living* has truly enhanced my life. Thank you.

Al Romas

Glenn's *Simple Thoughts About Life and Living* have had an incredible effect on my daily life. Each time I read them, I feel as though he is writing/speaking directly to me. They have helped me realize that our lives are so special and that we can make a difference in others' lives, as well. I hope that Glenn continues to guide all of us with his wonderful insight and wisdom.

Evelyn Brown

Each day as I drive to work I remember the meaning of the "words" you have sent me… "Think positive, think of the good in your life, remember the best, focus on the good…etc…of all that is good." I thank you, and I listen to all you've sent me each and every day. Your words are not just "words"; they are a part of my life.

Doreen, Lindenhurst, NY

I look forward to my daily *Simple Thoughts About Life & Living* e-mails. They are always expressed so well, and always make me think about my life and reflect, and even more so, give me a whole new perspective on my life and my actions. I often save the ones that I especially relate to, and please always keep them coming. They always give me pause for reflection, and even more importantly some introspection.

Warmest Regards, Rich Gallagher

Simple Thoughts About Perception

It's better to use your mind to create feelings of self-worth than to use your mind to create feelings of inadequacy.... simple stuff.

If you're stuck in a circumstance you want to change, it's a wise idea to begin by changing the patterns of your thoughts. If you think the same thoughts, say the same words, keep the same routines, your life will remain the same.

Changing the way you are looking at an "unsolvable" problem will often offer you the solution you've not been able to see…think about that.

Glenn Poveromo

You can't have a strong mind if you consistently allow it to dwell upon thoughts of weakness; however you can have a strong mind if you condition it to consistently dwell upon thoughts of strength.

Here's proof of Einstein's theory of relativity. A red light seems to last forever when you are stopped there and in a hurry to get somewhere. A red light seems to turn green much too quickly when it offers the opportunity for a long kiss with someone who excites you. Same red light, same duration of time, different way of perceiving it….simple stuff.

We all have a self-talk dialogue going on in our heads; it's just the way our minds work. We can use this self-talk to either build or beat ourselves up. What we say to ourselves is always a choice and has such a powerful effect on how we feel and perform.

Doors of discovery will fly open when you close the door on fear of failure…it's true!

The more energy you use to focus on what you don't have and what is wrong with your life, the less energy you will have to focus on what is good in your life and what is yours to enjoy…think about that.

Glenn Poveromo

The only things that can really bother you in life are the things you allow to really bother you...think about that.

It sure feels good to be respected and valued by others, but it feels even better to be respected and valued by yourself.

Your mind can be your greatest ally or your greatest enemy. It all depends on how you condition it and use it.

Not having the time to take care of your body and your mind is really an excuse for not *making* the time to do so. The age-old adage, "Where there's a will, there's a way" may indeed be very old, however, to this day, it is still very true.

The things that are usually the most difficult for us to do are the things that we make most difficult in our mind.

When you learn to master your thoughts you learn to master your life. That is why learning to consciously choose your thoughts is an essential ingredient to creating your best life possible.

Glenn Poveromo

Your head can hold an infinite amount of visions and dreams; however it's the amount of desire that you hold in your heart that will make any of them come true.

When I'm feeling hassled, frazzled, and upset I take some deep breaths and remind myself to move gracefully. This changes my rhythms and the hassles, frazzles, and upsets begin to subside. Try this when you are feeling that way…it works!

Those who go from rags to riches are those who have a deep desire to shed those rags and search in earnest for ways to make life a better experience. Those who remain in rags are those who accept that they have no other choice but to continue to wear them.

Simple Thoughts About Life & Living

We are blessed to live in a free country yet so many people are held prisoners by the limiting and self-defeating thoughts that they entertain in their mind…think about that.

Most of the limitations you believe you have are merely the result of what you've instructed your mind to believe. When you change your thinking you will change your believing; when you change your believing you will change your life.

People who have touched your life in a special way will remain in your soul forever. Those whose life you have touched in a special way will carry you in their souls as well.

You will not outperform your beliefs. If you believe you can't…you will find a way to fail. If you believe you can…you will find a way to succeed. The way to improve your performance is to improve your patterns of thinking…simple stuff.

Living in a cluttered material world can certainly make life difficult, but living in a cluttered mental world makes life more difficult still. A mind that races with anxiety, fear, guilt, worry, deadlines, difficult relationships, etc. is a mind that is depleted of focused energy. Take some time each day to relax your mind and clear the clutter…it makes for a better day.

We don't always get what we want, but we almost always get what we expect. When you learn to raise your expectations you learn to get more of what you want…think about that!

You could probably come up with a plethora of reasons about why you can't make your dream(s) come true. If you take the time to analyze each one it's likely that most, if not all, will really be excuses that are masking your fear of trying.

Both the "I can" and the "I can't" attitudes greatly affect how you will live your life and how you feel about yourself. Each attitude is shaped by the thoughts you allow your mind to think…think about that.

Glenn Poveromo

Those who make the impossible become possible are those who refuse to surrender their dream. They don't listen to those who tell them, "You can't;" they listen only to their inner voice that says, "I will."

You can't always get what you want, but you can always appreciate what you've got…simple stuff.

Many people think big but those who make their big dreams come true are those who believe big and take action…simple stuff.

The next time you find yourself all hassled and upset by things you've "got" to do, take a deep breath and think of them as things you "get" to do. There are millions and millions of people on this earth who would trade places with you in the blink of an eye…think about that!

Your thoughts can be your jailor, holding you captive to limiting expectations, or your thoughts can be your liberator, freeing you to create positive outcomes in your life. It's up to you to decide which thoughts you condition your mind to think.

When you create new patterns of thought in your life you create new patterns of living your life.

The more you speak to your mind about possibilities, the more possibilities your mind will seek. The more you speak to your mind about limitations, the more limitations your mind will accept.

Sing as often as you can, even if it's just in the shower or the car. It's not the sound of the song that matters; it's the feeling you get from singing that matters the most!

Most of the time we say, "I can't" is not because we really can't. We most often say, "I can't" because we're really afraid to try.

The saying that when one door closes another opens really is true. The problem many people have in finding this new door is that they remain at the closed one trying so hard to get back in. You can only find that new door if you walk away from the old one with open eyes and faith in finding it.

When my niece Sydney was eight years old she told me something I've never forgotten. She said, "Uncle Glenn, if you think happy…you'll feel happy." Thank you for the lesson Sydney; it's such a simple yet powerful truth.

Speak to yourself with dignity, respect, and positive statements of strength. The more you do, the more your mind will believe you. And once you truly believe, you will be exactly what you've created in your mind...think about that!

An old chair can be a piece of junk to one person or a treasure to another. It's all about how it's perceived. It's the same about life. Some see it as a chore filled with limitations, while others see it as a journey of possibilities and challenges. How you perceive life is entirely up to you. Simple stuff!

People can inspire faith in you; stay close to those who do so. But the faith that will allow you to move mountains is the faith that you have in yourself.

There are many people in life who accomplish so much more than others think they are capable of accomplishing. These special people are often labeled "overachievers." That is not the truth. They really are not overachievers; what they really are is fervent believers. They see themselves achieving and believe with all their heart that they will succeed. And that's why they do so!

Both the daydreamer and the person who accomplishes things have many creative thoughts and visions. The difference between the two is that the person who accomplishes things takes action…the daydreamer simply moves on to the next lofty dream.

Here's one to think about: When you think change is possible it might be. When you believe change is possible…it is!

The ordinary thinker hears of a tragedy and decides that he or she will get life in perspective and does so for a short period of time, but will eventually slip back into taking life for granted. The wise thinker keeps life in perspective each and every day…think about that.

Simple Thoughts About Life & Living

Your physical size doesn't make you big or small; what determines your true size is the size of the thoughts you condition your mind to think and the amount of desire you carry in your heart...simple stuff!

Simple Thoughts About Choice

You can be a slave to your thoughts or you can be the master of your thoughts…It's all how you choose to condition your mind to think.

When you have to wait in a doctor's office for an inordinate amount of time you can choose to read, listen to music, learn, study, etc. or you can choose to be angry, restless, agitated, and annoyed. Same amount of waiting, different way of spending it…think about that.

When you understand that you can consciously choose your thoughts you will truly understand the power of your mind.

We all have a self-talk dialogue going on in our heads; it's just the way our minds work. We can use this self-talk to either build or beat ourselves up. What we say to ourselves is always a choice and has such a powerful effect on how we feel and perform.

The more difficult you choose to make things in your mind the more difficult they will become in your reality. The less difficult you choose to make things in your mind the less difficult they will become in your reality as well…simple stuff.

Stress by itself will not hurt you. The harmful effects of stress are found in the way we choose to respond to it. Think about that.

One of the greatest advantages of learning to consciously choose your thoughts is that you can choose to dwell upon thoughts that make you feel good rather than choosing to dwell upon thoughts that make you feel poorly.

You can choose to spend your thinking time thinking of all the ways you are special or you can choose to spend your thinking time thinking of all the ways you are not. One will make you feel good, the other poorly. It's a wise idea to choose those that make you feel good...why not?

All kinds of thoughts will pop into your head during the course of a day. It is the thoughts you choose to entertain that will determine whether you will have a good feeling or a bad feeling day.

An "I can't" mind is filled with excuses for taking no action; an "I can" mind is filled with reasons for taking action. Both are states of mind that are produced by patterns of thought and when we learn to consciously choose our thoughts the "I can't" mind becomes capable of being transformed into an "I can" mind.

It's a wise idea to choose to speak to yourself as often as you can about the things you do best. It's a conversation that will make you feel a whole lot better than speaking to yourself about what you are not very good at.

You cannot always choose your circumstances but you can always choose your attitude toward them.

When pressed for time you can choose to allow yourself to become frustrated and unraveled, or you can choose to move gracefully. It's the same moment in time, just different ways of moving through it…simple stuff.

When you learn to consciously choose your thoughts you become empowered to let go of thoughts that trouble you and hold on to thoughts that make you feel uplifted and good. You understand that it's your thinking time and you can spend it thinking whatever thoughts you choose.

A mind that has been conditioned to fail will sabotage successes and ultimately find ways to fail. A mind that has been conditioned to succeed will regard failures as opportunities to refocus and ultimately find ways to succeed. When we learn that thoughts truly are choices we become empowered to consciously program our mind for success.

We all experience anger and resentment from time to time; it's a part of being human. Those who choose to release them live a happier life than those who choose to hold on…think about that.

You can train your mind to be problem oriented, focusing on problems, or solution oriented, focusing on solutions. Whichever you choose will have a huge impact on how you feel and how you live.

Our feelings of self-worth or lack of self-worth are the product of the thoughts we think in our minds. When we learn to consciously choose our thoughts we are capable of elevating our feeling of self-worth. Doing so will make life a happier and more fulfilling journey.

Choosing to dwell upon thoughts that make you smile will make you feel a whole lot better than choosing to dwell upon thoughts that make you frown.

Glenn Poveromo

If you choose to dwell upon thoughts that make you feel weak, you will feel weak. If you choose to dwell upon thoughts that make you feel anxious, you will feel anxious. If you choose to dwell upon thoughts that make you feel strong, you will feel strong. We are what we allow our minds to think.

Negative and troubling thoughts will enter your mind from time to time; it's just the way it is. However, the longer you choose to entertain and dwell upon them, the longer they will last and the larger they will become.

You are free to make healthy food choices. You are also free to make healthy thought choices…simple stuff.

Simple Thoughts About Life & Living

There are many successful people who were told by others that they were not big enough, strong enough, smart enough, etc. to succeed. These are people who chose to listen to their passion rather than the limiting words of others.

Those who choose to entertain peaceful thoughts will experience so many more happy moments in life than do those who choose to entertain troubling thoughts…simple stuff.

Happiness is not a physical object that can be purchased in a store. Happiness is a state of mind created by the thoughts you choose and the way you condition your mind to think.

When you come to understand that you can *choose* whatever thoughts you wish to think rather than *having* to think the thoughts you are used to thinking, life becomes an entirely new experience in thinking, perceiving, and living.

The amount of happiness or unhappiness you experience in life is a direct reflection of the thoughts you've conditioned your mind to think. You can recondition your mind at any moment in time…if you choose to. Think about that!

Your thoughts can make you a prisoner or your thoughts can set you free. It all depends upon the thoughts you choose to think…simple stuff.

Those who focus their attention on their blessings seem to attract more blessings into their life. Those who focus their attention on their problems seem to attract more problems into their life. We are free to focus our attention anywhere we choose…hmmm.

Everyone comes to a wall at some time; it's just the way of life. When this happens you can allow it to stop you from moving forward or you can do whatever it takes to get to the other side. The choice is always yours.

Happy people focus upon what they like about themselves and what's good in their lives. Unhappy people focus upon their weaknesses and what they lack in life. Both perceptions will affect how you spend your valuable living time and both perceptions are choices.

We have all heard of the power of positive thinking but we don't hear much about the power of negative thinking. Entertaining this power will erode you mind, body, and spirit. We are always free to choose either negative or positive thoughts. Which do you choose for yourself? Think about that.

The most secure people in this world are those who don't focus on comparing themselves to others and the things they perceive they lack. They choose to focus on their blessings, strengths, and all that makes them special.

A steady diet of junk food and negative thinking might seem harmless in the moment, but both will hurt you in the long run. If you want to live your best life possible, be careful about what you choose to put into your body and your mind.

Procrastination is a choice…simple stuff.

Choosing thoughts of love makes the world look a whole lot different than choosing thoughts of anger. It's the same planet you're walking upon; it's just the way you're choosing to see it.

There are many things in life that we can choose and many things in life we cannot choose. However one thing we can consistently choose are our thoughts; doing so is empowering.

The more difficult you choose to make things in your mind the more difficult they will become in your reality. The same is true for choosing to make them simpler…think about that.

Failures and disappointments often happen in life, it's just the way it is. If we choose to hold on to them they will become empowered to bring us pain, frustration, and a loss of valuable living time. If we choose to release them and look in a different direction, they then become opportunities to gain strength and discover new ways of thinking and doing.

An optimist chooses to perceive life as a journey of lessons and possibilities. A pessimist chooses to perceive life as an existence of trials and limitations. Which do you suppose lives a happier and more fulfilling life? Think about that!

If you focus primarily upon your pain, then life will be painful. If you focus primarily upon your joy, then life will be joyful. It really is a matter of choice!

Positive thoughts instruct the brain to release healing hormones into your body. They make you feel good. Negative thoughts instruct the brain to release stress hormones into your body. They make you feel bad. Thoughts are always choices. Hmmm… this is one to think about!

How you think has a powerful influence upon how you feel. It's a wise idea to choose thoughts that make you feel good…simple stuff.

Simple Thoughts About Peace, Love, Kindness, and Friendship

Simple Thoughts About Life & Living

A peaceful mind lives an entirely different life than does a troubled mind. Our entire perception of people, places, and things are colored by our state of mind. And our state of mind does much to influence the people and experiences we attract into our lives. Life is so interesting if you allow it to be so!

Life can be lived in so many different ways. Those who live with happiness in their minds, hearts, and souls are those who live a life well lived.

The more anxiety you release from your mind the more room you create for peaceful thoughts to dwell there...simple stuff.

Those who truly care for you will make the time to be there for you. Those who don't truly care will make excuses why they can't. Value those who truly care and be sure to be there for them too.

Life can be lived in so many different ways. Those who live with happiness in their minds, hearts, and souls experience an entirely different life than those who do not.

What every person wants in the deepest part of him/herself is to be happy, to live a purposeful and fulfilling life, and to love and be loved...I wish these things for you.

There are many people who will enter our life that we are happy to know and they will eventually move on. However, those who enter our souls remain there forever and neither time nor distance will ever change that. Cherish those who live within your soul and simply love them.

Glenn Poveromo

One of the greatest gifts and simplest acts of kindness you can offer a friend in need is to help them ease their troubled mind.

Pay attention to your heart. Our mind creates many wonderful visions of how we'd like life to be, but it's our heart that gives us the passion, desire, and energy to make our dreams come true...think about that.

A peaceful mind thinks in terms of possibilities. A troubled mind thinks in terms of limitations. I wish you a peaceful mind.

My grandchildren are very young. They will not be impressed by the size of someone's house, their car, clothing, or money. What will make an impression upon them is a person's kindness and attentiveness. Thanks, Max and Mia, you help to keep your grandpa grounded.

A troubled mind can be aware of its blessings but unable to fully appreciate and enjoy them. A peaceful mind is aware of its blessings and appreciates and enjoys them to the fullest. I wish you a peaceful mind.

You can forgive others in your mind, however true forgiveness occurs when you forgive in your heart.

Casual friends are usually abundant in life, but true friends are often rare and always special. Be sure to let your true friends know that they are loved and appreciated…it's an important thing to do.

Extending simple acts of kindness toward others is a great way to add some positive energy to this world. Give it a shot…the world sure can use it!

Forgiving is often difficult to do however it frees you from anger, anxiety, and pain…think about that.

Those who offer selfless acts of kindness and love do not feel a need to be recognized for doing so; they simply feel a need to make the life of another better in some way.

The reason why you can see an old friend whom you've not seen in a long while and feel like no time has passed is because love knows no time, distance, or conditions…love is simply love.

Glenn Poveromo

When you touch someone's heart through the power of love and kindness you will remain somewhere in their heart forever…it's just the way it is.

A peaceful heart and an anxious heart offer you completely different rhythms. Both are the product of the thoughts you allow your mind to think…I wish you a peaceful heart.

Holding my baby grandchildren in my arms while they are sleeping is one of the greatest thrills I've ever known. It doesn't matter where we are, how much money is in my pocket, or whether it's a sunny or rainy day. It's just the simple power of love that feels so mighty fine…I wish you love.

Your success and prosperity in your outer world won't be fully enjoyed and appreciated unless you are at peace in your inner world. I wish you peace.

Compassion is not unique to any race, ethnicity, or creed. Nor is compassion unique to any socio-economic or educational group. Compassion is simply the part of one's soul that heeds the call to help others in need.

Kindness is among the greatest gifts you can offer anyone. It need not cost money; it need only be a gesture from your heart. Extend kindness toward others and be sure to extend it toward yourself as well.

There is no success greater than attaining peace of mind. A peaceful mind wants for nothing and appreciates all that it has…simple stuff.

There might not be many places in your physical environment that offer you a peaceful and quiet opportunity to relax, but you can always find a place of peace and quiet in your mind. Try to find some time each day to just be you.

When you're feeling peace in your heart and soul life seems to flow more easily. Do you know what brings peace into your heart and soul? Spend some time thinking about that today.

Simple Thoughts About Life & Living

There will be many people who are friendly with you, will share a time in life with you, and then they will move on, but a true friend remains a part of your life forever. Time, space, and circumstance might separate you but somehow, some way, you'll find a way to remain united.

When you learn to create peace and harmony in your mind you learn to create peace and harmony in your reality…simple stuff.

Helping someone who feels awkward and uncomfortable to feel more secure is a very simple yet very powerful act of kindness…think about that!

A peaceful mind is not guaranteed a longer life than a troubled mind, but a peaceful mind is guaranteed a happier journey. I wish you peace.

Sometimes we hurt the people we love, sometimes the people we love hurt us. That happens in relationships from time to time. But if you focus more on the love that binds you and less on the pain of the moment, then forgiveness will bridge the gap of pain and bring you back to harmony.

The gift of simple kindness, with nothing expected in return, is among the greatest gifts that anyone could either give or receive.

The most powerful drug that exists on this planet is the feeling of love. You don't need a doctor's authorization, there is no co-pay or fee, and there are no therapist services involved. All it takes to fill this prescription is the connection of one heart to another…I wish you love!

Glenn Poveromo

A peaceful mind opens your eyes to so many things that a troubled, anxious, or angry mind is just not able to see. I wish you a peaceful mind.

We gain peace when we surrender our anxiety...think about that!

I believe that the Beatles got it right when they sang:
"And in the end, the love you take
Is equal to the love you make."
I wish you love…

It doesn't take a lot of money, status, or possessions to show kindness toward others. All it takes is the desire in one's heart to help make another's life just a little bit better in some way...

True beauty lives within. When you feel beautiful, you carry yourself with beauty. When you feel beautiful inside, it radiates outward. Your true beauty is not the product of your physical features; your true beauty is the reflection of the beauty that lives within your heart and soul.

Glenn Poveromo

Praying for peace is a good thing to do, but actually extending peace toward others is even better.

If you have a friend who is experiencing a difficult moment in life, offer them your ear and really hear them. Don't judge, just truly listen. Chances are they won't be looking for your advice, only your attention and compassion to help them along their way.

There are special people in this world who selflessly help others for no other reason except kindness…you can be one too!

Simple Thoughts About Life & Living

When giving a gift it's not the size of the package or the size of the price tag that matters. What matters most is the size of the love with which it is given.

Some people say you can create love through magic. I'm not entirely sure if that's true. Maybe it is, maybe it isn't. But I am sure of one thing: Once you find love and it fills your heart and soul….the whole world becomes magic. I wish you love!

Simple Thoughts About Positive Thinking

Positive thinking may or may not completely change your circumstances, but one thing it will definitely do is help you to live your life a little more happily and a little more securely.

The more you speak to and about yourself in a discouraging and limited way the more likely you will live your life in a limited and discouraging way. The more you speak to yourself in a positive and limitless way the more likely you are to live your life in a positive and limitless way.

Positive people don't always experience the best of circumstances but they try to make the best of whatever their circumstances might be…simple stuff!

Positive people are a whole lot more comfortable to be around than negative people. How do people feel about you?

Consistently speaking to yourself in a positive way is a powerful tool for developing a positive outlook on life…think about that.

Simple Thoughts About Life & Living

Here are four thoughts to consider about conditioning your mind to think in a positive way:

1. Positive thinking won't guarantee a perfect life, but it will guarantee more perfect moments to enter your life.

2. Positive thinking won't guarantee a stress-free life, but it will guarantee less stressful moments in your life.

3. Positive thinking won't guarantee that difficult moments won't occur in your life, but it will guarantee that you will move through them more gracefully and focus on solutions rather than the difficulties.

4. Positive thinking won't guarantee a longer life, but it will guarantee a happier and more fulfilling journey filled with thoughts of possibility.

The more negative and limiting thoughts that you clear from your mind, the more room you'll create for positive and limitless thoughts to fill it...that's powerful.

Don't spend too much time around negative people...you might become one too! Seek companions who are positive...it will help to make your life a more pleasant and productive journey!

Positive thinking may or may not completely change your circumstances but one thing it will definitely do is help you to live your life a little more happily and a little more securely…simple stuff.

The people and circumstances you will attract into your life through a positive mind that dwells on possibilities are likely to be different from the people and circumstances you will attract into your life through a negative mind that dwells on limitations...think about that.

It's a wise idea to surround yourself with positive people. The more positive people you include in your life, the more positive ideas and perceptions will enter your mind. The more positive ideas and perceptions that you entertain in your mind, the more positive outcomes you will attract into your life.

Whenever I find myself becoming mired in negative thoughts I stop and ask myself, "Are these thoughts helping me? Do I have to keep thinking them?" The answer is always "no" and this helps me transform my thinking time from negative to positive. Try it, it works!

Positive people see the impossible and ask how it can become possible. Negative people see the impossible and accept that it is so.

It's not always easy to remain positive in a difficult moment in time, but those who have learned to do so usually pass through the moment more quickly and emerge from this moment with a greater strength in character.

You speak to your mind constantly; your mind is consistently filled with self-talk conversation. If you choose to eliminate that negative voice and replace it with a positive dialogue, your life will become a more positive experience...think about that!

The more you practice thinking positive thoughts the better you'll become at it and the better your life will be. It won't necessarily change the ways of the world, but it will change the way you perceive them...think about that!

If you go to the gym faithfully for a few months straight you will begin to notice a difference in your strength and your body's shape. If you practice positive thinking faithfully for a few months straight you will notice a difference in how you perceive and respond to life's circumstances...simple stuff!

Think of thoughts as guests you've invited into your mind to spend some time with you. Would you rather spend your time with negative or positive guests? Whichever you choose... you've invited them. Think about that!

Words are so powerful! They can actually alter the course of one's thinking, which alters the course of one's actions. That's why it's important to speak positive and uplifting words to someone very special... yourself!

Glenn Poveromo

Learning to think positively won't guarantee a stress free life, but it will help you move through moments of stress more gracefully and provide your mind with solutions to relieve what is stressing you.

Our minds are like a garden. Whatever seeds we place in them are the plants that will grow. If you tend your garden with positive thoughts, then positive outcomes will grow. If you tend your garden with limiting and negative thoughts, you'll likely get weeds.
Give this one some thought!

One of the "secrets" to living a positive life is to surround yourself with positive people. If you can't find them in the flesh then find them in books, movies... anywhere you can. It will just make your life a more interesting and pleasant experience.

Thinking positive or negative thoughts is a choice each of us makes. Positive people see setbacks as a temporary situation. They'll use the power of their mind to find a way to get them back on the path of success.

Those who condition their minds to think in a positive direction will live a different reality than those who condition their minds to think in a negative direction...think about that.

Surround yourself with positive people; it will help to bring out the best in you… it will help you bring out the best in others as well. Think about that!

Do you know people who inspire positive thoughts and feelings within you? If so, stay close to them…stay inspired!

It would be nice to think that by merely thinking positive thoughts your life will be perfect, but life doesn't happen that way. However, thinking positive thoughts will create more perfect moments than thinking negative thoughts…simple stuff.

Do you know what's cool about practicing positive thinking? You don't have to go to the gym; you don't have to run for miles. All you have to do is focus on thinking positive thoughts. And it's these positive thoughts that will get you to the gym, through your toughest moments, or wherever you wish to go. Simple stuff...but very, very true!

A negative mind has only occasional moments of peace. A positive mind has only occasional moments of negativity. How have you conditioned your mind to think?

In any moment you can choose to think in a positive or negative direction. Which do you most often do?

Glenn Poveromo

The advantages of choosing to think positively can certainly be debated, but one thing is certain. Choosing to dwell upon positive thoughts will make you feel a whole lot better than choosing to dwell upon negative thoughts… simple stuff.

Sometimes you have to do things you don't feel like doing, but you still have to get them done. When this happens, keep in mind you can do them with either a positive or negative attitude; your choice will affect your entire experience.

Positive thoughts instruct your brain to release healing hormones into your body; they make you feel good. Negative thoughts instruct your brain to release stress hormones into your body; they make you feel bad. Hmmm…one to think about.

Living your life with negative thoughts of "I can't" is entirely different than living your life with positive thoughts of "I can." You can condition your mind to think in either direction and whichever you do will have a direct influence on how your life will be…think about that.

A positive thinking person will be having a bad day but remind him/herself that somehow things will get better. A negative thinking person will be having a good day but remind him/herself that somehow things will go wrong. Both states of mind will affect how we feel and live.

We have learned to practice so many things in our lives! We have learned to practice for sports, for performances, for exams, etc. Yet how many of us have actually learned to practice thinking positive thoughts? Give it a shot...it just might make a powerful change within you.

It's just as easy to think a positive thought as it is to think a negative thought…simple stuff.

If you're going to spend a lot of time thinking about things you might as well spend your thinking time with positive thoughts and thoughts of possibilities rather than thoughts of lament and limits. Same amount of thinking, different way of thinking and feeling.

The best way to create a positive thinking habit is to constantly remind yourself that you are free to do so…think about that.

Glenn Poveromo

No one in the recorded history of the world has lived upon this earth forever. It's not likely that you or I will be the first to do so. That's why it's a good idea to enjoy life as much as you can while it's your turn to live. Learning to develop a positive outlook and choosing thoughts that do so will make life a more pleasant experience.

Simple Thoughts About
Thinking Time
Living Time
Life As A Journey

Spending your thinking time focusing on possibilities and blessings will make you feel a whole lot better than spending your thinking time focusing on limitations and problems. It's your thinking time; you are free to spend it focusing on whatever thoughts you choose.

In any situation, you can dwell upon thoughts of the worst possible scenario or thoughts of the best possible scenario. It's your thinking time; you can spend it dwelling upon any thoughts you choose.

You can use your thinking time to create feelings of self-worth, or you can use your thinking time to create feelings of inadequacy. Same thinking time, different way of spending it.

This is your living time and it is precious. When you fritter away any of this valuable time stressing over things that you make more important in your mind than they are in reality, you've wasted valuable living time that cannot be reclaimed...think about that.

We all experience disappointments and hurts from time to time, life is just that way. Those who dwell upon their disappointments for long periods of time waste a lot of valuable living time that cannot be regained. Those who accept what made them disappointed and move on in a new direction have more living time to enjoy.

Life consists of moments in time and in any moment you live you are capable of making the best or worst of it...simple stuff.

Spending your living time focusing upon all that you can do well will feel a whole lot better than focusing upon all you cannot do well. Your living time is precious…why not choose to spend it feeling the best way you possibly can?

This is your living time and it's important to do the things you *have* to do, yet it's important to do the things you *love* to do as well.

When you let go of grudges and resentment you make room for better thoughts and feelings to enter your mind and heart, which ultimately makes for a stronger, happier, and more fulfilling journey…think about that.

When you make a big deal over little things they sometimes become so big that they absorb way too much of your thinking and living time that could be spent in better ways had you kept them in perspective and just moved on…simple stuff.

Those who have conditioned their minds to perceive life as a privilege have an entirely different living experience than those who have conditioned their minds to perceive life as a chore.

Many people give up on their goals and dreams because it takes them beyond the safety of their comfort zone. If you practice doing things beyond your comfort zone of safety on a regular basis you will create a new comfort zone of daring to try, which will make life an entirely different journey.

If you have a pair of eyes that allow you to see, ears that allow you to hear, arms, legs, hands, and feet that allow you to move, then you possess incredible blessings that money cannot buy. It's a wise idea to take time to appreciate them while they are yours to enjoy.

You can spend your thinking time focusing on either negative or positive thoughts. Each will influence how you feel. A wise choice is to opt for thoughts that make you feel good. This is your living time; why not create as many moments of feeling good as you possibly can?

Making a positive difference in this world is a fine way to journey through life. It matters not how large or small your contribution might be, only that you make a difference.

Life without a dream in your heart can be a good life, but life with a dream burning in your heart is a great life. Dare to dream…it's a great way to spend your living time.

Life can change in the blink of an eye and everything can become so very different. That's why it's a wise idea to enjoy and appreciate all that's yours to enjoy and appreciate before life might make you blink.

Life is so interesting because there are so many ways it can be lived and perceived. A great skill to master is to learn to be peaceful in your heart and mind, no matter what circumstances life might either offer you or impose upon you. A peaceful heart and a satisfied mind make life a fulfilling journey.

If you constantly make a big deal over little things, you'll likely waste your highly valuable living time being overwhelmed by "big deals" that are really not so big at all…think about that.

This is your living time, your turn to live. How happily or unhappily you spend it depends upon the thoughts you allow your mind to think.

If you spend today focusing upon negative and limiting thoughts then you are wasting a day of living time that you can never get back…think about that!

It's a wise idea to spend some thinking time each day focusing on all that you are grateful for. It will make you feel a whole lot different than spending that same thinking time focusing on all that you lack…simple stuff.

When you arrive at the perception that life on this planet is a finite experience and you have x amount of days to live you'll stop wasting time being upset over trivial matters and circumstances. This is your living time…use it to create your best life possible.

Fixating on a grudge you hold against someone hurts you more than it hurts them because it's your body that is experiencing the consequences of the stress, anger, and frustration it creates. It also steals valuable living time that could be spent thinking of ways to make your life more peaceful and productive.

Each morning that I wake up in a safe, warm, and comfortable bed I feel a deep feeling of appreciation, for I know there are millions of others on this earth who do not have this simple blessing to enjoy. If life is being kind to you at this moment in time, be sure to enjoy all that is yours to enjoy while it's still your turn to enjoy it.

I used to spend a lot of time worrying about the future until I realized that I was wasting a lot of valuable living time focusing on things that would likely never even come to pass. How about you?

The essence of life is not so much about how long you live; the essence of life is about how well you live while it's your turn to be alive.

We know the day we are born into this world but we don't know the day we will depart from it. This being so, any moments spent on needless fear and anxiety are wasted moments that could have been better spent on creating a more positive experience on this finite journey of life.

How and where you spend your moments in time isn't always up to you, but the mindset in which you spend them is always up to you…think about that!

Simple Thoughts About Life & Living

When you take a moment to consider that all people, including yourself, will one day leave this planet, it makes the time spent on anxiety and negative thinking seem like such a waste of valuable living time that could be spent in better and more productive ways.

Wasting money is not a wise thing to do. However, wasting your living time by constantly thinking negative thoughts and all the things you lack is the biggest waste of all.

Many times when I drive by a cemetery I wonder how many souls resting there regret not what they've done in life, rather they regret what they've been afraid to try.

Glenn Poveromo

The next time you're feeling down, anxious, or upset in any way, take some time to listen to and feel your breath. It will remind you that you're alive, and as long as you have breath in your body you have the potential to rise to better circumstances.

The only certainty that any of us have is that one day we will leave this earth. This is not meant to be a morbid statement, but rather a reminder that we should celebrate our life while it is ours to live. Find as much peace and joy as you possibly can; find ways to smile in your heart. Move past any barriers your mind has created; live your dreams and be moved by your passions. Perceive life as a very interesting and special journey and that is exactly what it will be.

Think of how you'd like to be remembered once your life is through, then turn around and live that description so your life will truly be remembered that way!

None of us will live on this earth forever, that's a fact. That's why it's kind of foolish to spend our time here being hard on ourselves and negative in our minds. Try to celebrate your life while it's still yours to live. Think about that!

You can live your life as a journey that is filled with ups, downs, tears, and joy, or you can live your life as a chore.

There are moments we've lived in the past, but we can no longer live them. We can project future moments and visualize how they might be, but we cannot yet live them. The only moment we can truly live, with all of our might, is the moment we are in right now.

Life is simply now. It doesn't matter where you're going or where you've been…it's only *now* that matters.

No one gets out of life alive. While you are here you can just live or you can be alive with dreams and passion. Think about that.

Final Thought

I hope that the thoughts contained within this book will help to uplift some people; I hope those uplifted people will help to uplift other people, and they in turn will uplift others as well. It can be done with some simple thoughts…that's all it really takes.

Wishing you Peace, Love, & a Smile in your Heart….

Glenn Poveromo is a motivational teacher and life coach. He teaches people to understand how to utilize the inherent power of their mind in order to live their best life possible. He has authored *The Spirit's Self-Help Book* and *Change Your Thinking/Change Your Life...Learn To Live Your Best Life Possible*. He has also created an audio CD *Glennisms: Simple Thoughts About Life & Living* and shares these thoughts each Monday, Wednesday, and Friday with thousands of people via his web site.

Glenn's company, *The Power of Visualization*, offers clients the mental tools to be used in creating positive outcomes in all areas of their lives. His desire is to help people to utilize both their spiritual and mental abilities to help individuals experience life as a fulfilling existence, and to create a more peaceful, harmonious world.

If you are interested in receiving Glenn's *Thought For The Day* you can subscribe by visiting: www.thepov.net, or contact Glenn at: creatingstrength@aol.com.

www.ingramcontent.com/pod-product-compliance
Lightning Source LLC
Chambersburg PA
CBHW061454040426
42450CB00007B/1359